Pickleball Doubles

Master the Fastest Growing Game of America with Exact Tips, Techniques, and Advance Double Strategies to Win the Game with Your Partner

Dennis Hall

Contents

Introduction

Pickleball is America's fastest-growing sport. It has over 2.8 million gamers globally (and counting), so now is the time to jump on board. It's a low-impact, recreational sport that's appropriate for people of all ages. Pickleball winners were awarded in age groups ranging from 19 to 75 years and older during the just concluded US Open.

This book will teach you the tactics that virtually all top tournament players utilize to win and master doubles Pickleball. If you follow this basic shot-by-shot tutorial, you will be able to improve your game swiftly.

In summary, the tactic is getting your team as close to the non-volley zone (NVZ) line as possible, and then ideally playing out the rally while staying near the NVZ line. Furthermore, the approach entails attempting to keep your opponent's away from the NVZ line. As easy as playing at the line appears, it is more complicated than this. It can be difficult to get to the line when your opponents are smashing the ball at your feet, and it can all be lost if your opponent's hit a smart lob shot.

Why is it so crucial to put your best foot forward? Being on the net gives you the most strategic edge. You have the most angles and positioning options to choose from. You may also hit the ball down on the ground. Furthermore, if you and your partner are linked, you can defend your side of the court better than if you are further back.

You have no option but to strive to progress to the NVZ line in competitive play. The statistic is as follows: if the enemy team is at the NVZ line and you cannot get your squad there, you have a 70% probability of losing the rally. It's as easy as this: whatever team controls the net, wins the game. The side that can get to the NVZ line faster and more consistently, and maintain dominance there for a longer period, will win the match. Data from competitive play certainly supports this.

This book will be useful to players who want to compete against other 'at-the-line' players. Please do not assume that the method outlined in this book does not apply to social play or matches with opponents who do not progress. It tackles how to handle most scenarios, including those involving deep players, middle-of-the-box players, heavy hitters (bangers), and lobbers, the method detailed in this book is completely appropriate to all levels of play. Even if you do not want to play forward at the line, this book will still be useful since it teaches you what to do when you are not at the line.

It is important to note that the at-the-line style of play will not occur unless all players are dedicated to playing fully forward and capable of going fully forward. The short dinking game, for example, should only take place when all players are completely forward. You should not invite a player forward by dinking to them if they are not fully forward, as you will learn later. Instead, try to keep them away from the NVZ line by placing the ball at foot depth, and in a spot that needs as much movement or stretching as feasible.

If you opt to play away from the net, you will employ the methods applicable to the midcourt or backcourt positions. As a result, the technique presented in this book will be useful to players of all skill levels because it tackles how to manage most scenarios. It is a complete plan that addresses every situation. However, some strategic features (for example, dinking) may be unnecessary against some sorts of opponents, such as those that never advance too far forward.

To be a great player, one must master more than just the at-the-line tactics. Making accurate shots and striking the ball with power and agility is a must for greatness on the court. This book will explain how to increase your strategy, ball-hitting, and shot-making skills.

So, to play superb Pickleball, you will need the following:

Mobility: Even top-level Pickleball players without exceptional mobility is practically impossible and playing 4.5-level Pickleball without strong mobility is nearly impossible. Even with limited mobility, you may be an excellent Pickleball player if you play wisely and have outstanding ball-striking and shot-making abilities.

Your Ball-Striking Ability: This is the ability to consistently obtain the desired hit and placement—that is, to eliminate flubs, mishits, and poor direction control.

Shot-Making Ability: This ability comes before ball-striking ability. This refers to your ability to make specialty shots that are incredibly difficult for your opponents to return. Among these specialty shots are steeply angled dink shots, lob shots, drop shots, and deception shots.

Strategic Plan and Shot-Selection Skill: That's where to be and how, and where to place the ball.

Chapter One

Pickleball Fundamentals

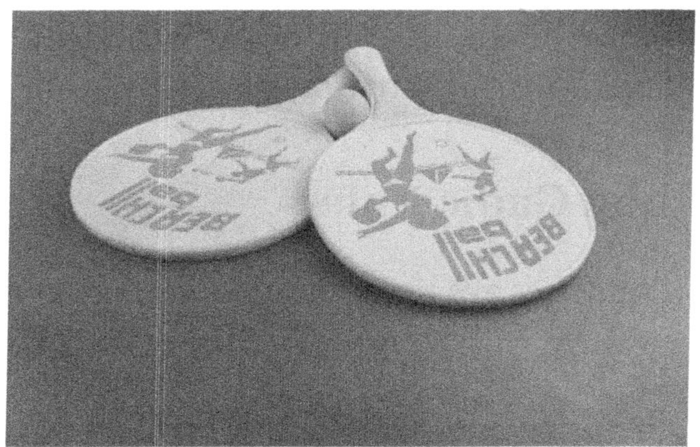

Pickleball can be a straightforward game if you keep the Pickleball above the net and between the court lines more than your opponents. And to do so, several fundamentals are necessary on the Pickleball court. Having two hands on the paddle before making the backswing for a ground stroke, or the punch in a volley, results in more precise ball striking. Most strokes in sports are more accurate when executed with two hands rather than one. For example, you do not need the power of both arms to putt a golf ball. On the other hand, your putting precision is significantly greater with two hands on the putter than with one. When shooting baskets with a basketball, you do not need to use both arms to make the shot. However, shooting with two hands is far more precise than firing with one. Sign painters will use two hands, not one, while hand painting a sign (assuming they are not utilizing a guide rail).

Doubles Game Rules

- Matches are best, winning two out of three games with a combined score of 11 points.
- You can only score a point when your team is serving.
- Serving has to be done underhand, and contact must be made below the waist.

- Serves must move diagonally and settle between the non-volley zone and the other court's baseline.

- Each player is limited to one (1) serving attempt. EXCEPTION: If the ball strikes the net and falls on the correct serving court, the serve is overturned.

- At the game start, only one player from the first serving side is permitted to serve before the ball is passed to the opponents. After that, each team member will have a service turn before the ball is given to the opposite team.

- When a serving team scores a point, the server goes to the other side of the court. The receiving team is never switched.

- The serving team score will be even when the player serves on the right side, and odd when the player serves on the left side.

- Each team must play its first shot off the bounce under the "double bounce rule!" The receiving team must allow the serve to bounce before playing it, and the serving team must allow the return of the serve to bounce before playing it. The ball can be played off the bounce or immediately out of the air after the first two bounces.

- Non-Volley Zone—A player cannot walk on or over the non-volley line after striking a volley. This results in their team losing the point.

- After hitting a volley, a player may leap across the non-volley line if they do not contact any section of the non-volley zone line when hitting the ball.

- On a team's side, the ball may only bounce once. The point is lost if there are many bounces.

Wall Practice

Understanding the strategy is simply one aspect of being a great player. One of the first things you'll need is ball-striking skills, or the ability to obtain the desired hit and placement consistently. To advance in Pickleball, you must limit errors, mishits, and shots that go in the incorrect direction. Practice time will improve player's skills at all levels more than playing time. Almost all sports follow this guideline. While playing is more enjoyable than training, it is a terribly ineffective approach to improving your skills.

When you play instead of practice, you don't get the chance to find out how to fix your problems, or perfect your shots.

In Pickleball, you can hit at least ten times more shots per hour utilizing a practice wall (a backboard) than you can in a game. You may also learn to direct the ball left and right, as well as volley, dink, serve, and hit various other shots. To mark the top of the net placement, apply painter's tape to the wall. Many people who read this will disregard this advice without hesitation. Their response is as follows:

- It's too boring: It would be too boring if you just hit the same shot repeatedly. As a result, you must work on dinks, forehand and backhand groundstrokes, forehand and backhand volleys, alternating forehand and backhand volleys, spin shots, serves, drop shots, and lobs.
- There isn't time for this: Because the efficiency factor is so high (more than ten times the hits per hour than playing time),

you need to spend fifteen minutes each day practicing this to improve your ability significantly.

- It isn't the same as playing, thus, it won't help: True, you don't get exposed to all the game conditions, but you also don't get to repeat shots and focus on certain demands in a real game. Practice enables you to take a shot and improve it over time.

The advantages of utilizing a practice wall will not appear quickly. However, your game will drastically improve within six months if you spend ten minutes every day practicing dinks, serves, drop shots, volleys, and so on. A skilled player should be able to strike a hundred or more consecutive volley shots without error against a wall.

Forehand and Backhand Strokes Practice

Shot by shot, let's look at the strokes that are used.

The serve is performed with an underhand stroke with the paddle's head below the wrist. You may generate a more linear paddle movement through the ball-hitting zone by bending your knees. Anyone experiencing difficulty with the serve should practice against a gymnasium wall. Mark the location of the top of the net with a strip of painter's tape. You may also practice on an unoccupied Pickleball court.

A regular forehand or backhand ground stroke would be employed to return the serve. The strategies for ground strokes in Pickleball and tennis are largely similar; however, there are two distinctions. Pickleball strokes must be shorter and more compact than tennis strokes because you must "reset" faster. Secondly, the ball in Pickleball demands more of a lifting or an upward stroke than in tennis.

The technique for a conventional ground stroke is as follows:

- First and foremost, get into position fast so you don't have to reach for the ball. The stance of a right-handed player hitting a forehand shot will be oriented so that the left shoulder and left foot are leading and are approaching the net.

- The angling is reversed for a right-handed player hitting a backhand shot. The paddle remains close to the player rather than

> being pushed off to the side. The backswing should come considerably before the forward swing. The paddle route is quite straight and goes from low to high through the striking zone. It's ideal to wait until the ball drops before attempting a ground stroke from deep in the court.

Almost all movement is generated by torso rotation and arm hinging at the shoulder. Wrist and elbow mobility account for almost negligible paddle movement. Movement from the shoulder produces a large radius and, as a result, a modest paddle path curvature. A blocking motion is approximated through the moment of contact when the paddle movement seeks to continue the same route as the ball for a long distance rather than abruptly swinging off the ball path. Small radius swings, such as those produced by flipping the wrist or snapping the elbow, obviously need tremendous timing precision and, consequently, provide inconsistent results. Poor stroke technique is the source of many unforced mistakes. Above all, consider raising or scooping the ball from beneath the ball while maintaining the swing path linear and close to your body.

Many skilled players prefer to add backspin to their return-of-serve shots to make their opponent's following, the crucial third shot, even more difficult. There is definitely merit in making your opponent's third shot tough. However, there are certain things to consider: can you routinely return serve shots with backspin at least halfway back on your opponent's serving courts? When returning serves in this manner, can you make it to the non-volley zone (NVZ) line on time? Don't try to chop downward if you add a backspin. On the other hand, the right paddle path is almost leveled through the stroke.

It is recommended to adopt the regular ground stroke previously outlined for the third shot (drop shot), striking the ball squarely and rising from underneath rather than attempting to impart spin. The typical drop shot stroke in tennis travels from high to low (a path shaped like a quarter moon) and imparts a backspin on the ball. Indeed, the backspin improves the ball's flight trajectory, causing the ball to float over the net. If you can consistently make such a spin shot, then go for it. However, glancing impacts (cut shots) need accuracy. The third shot is already difficult. Many instructors recommend employing a push shot on the third shot. Straightening the elbow and pushing the paddle forward along the planned route, with the bottom edge of the blade leading to give lift and some backspin, is how to make a backhand push shot. It's worth noting that this stroke employs blocking or linear motion rather than swinging. Ping-pong players should be familiar with this backhand push shot.

It is recommended to employ the typical groundstroke for most dink shots, striking the ball straight and from below, with most movement coming from the shoulder. On most dink shots, add a little backspin. Bend your knees, as with other shots, to get beneath the ball and generate a more linear paddle path. When you're standing straight up and trying to strike a ball at the level of your knees, it's very hard to eliminate paddle path curvature.

Volley Shots

Volley shots are typically employed when the fast game breaks out, and the majority of these will involve a backhand punch or push. A lightning-fast reaction time is essential. The greatest approach to improve this talent is backboard practice, alternating forehand and backhand volley shots.

Increase the speed and distance from the wall as you improve on the backboard. Try volleying into the wall as quickly as possible to increase your response time and game focus. With such wall practice, your rapid volley game will develop drastically in a short period.

Analysis

The return-of-serve shot is one area where there is a decent risk vs. reward ratio for employing a spin shot. Your opponents must allow the ball to bounce, meaning you have a vast open court to tolerate shot mistakes. Making a very brief response, which might incite hostility, is a mistake. Even for the return-of-serve shot, employ the spin shot only if you and your partner are committed to getting completely to the NVZ line by the time the third shot crosses the net (which you should be), forcing your opponent to make a key third shot. Making the crucial third shot as tough as possible has considerable advantages.

A wall is an excellent place to practice spin shot ground strokes. Alternate between forehand and backhand spin shot ground strokes. Almost all paddle action will occur from the shoulder, as with the typical ground stroke. Instead of being completely square to the planned ball route, the paddle face will be somewhat open at impact, with the paddle swing path shifting out to compensate. Because you hit from just behind the ball, the spin you impart will be a mix of backspin and sidespin.

Understand the Footwork

Split-Step

The Split-Step: watching elite players do the split-step may be easier to learn than reading an explanation. Watch the feet of the service receiver as they prepare to receive the serve if you are watching top Pickleball tournament players on YouTube, for example. The recipient does a split-step, which is a tiny jump onto split legs. This motion somewhat compresses or packs the legs, allowing for explosive movement. Furthermore, the pros nearly always repeat the split-step as their opponent is going to strike the ball. This action keeps you light and helps you to move quickly. Pickleball experts recommend that you split-step every time your opponents touch the ball, which might amount to several hundred split steps every game.

When approaching the NVZ line, how to complete the halt and split-step sequence

Halt and split-step: beginning with the third shot, the serving team must quickly move toward the NVZ line until they can establish themselves there. Unless you're lightning quick, you're unlikely to reach the NVZ line before the fourth shot returns to you. It is a mistake to continue charging forward when your opponent delivers the fourth shot. Instead, split-step as soon as your opponent smacks the ball and then gets squeezed. You may swiftly move left or right in this stopped-and-compressed stance, and you can bend forward to volley back shots coming at your feet. Running forward into a shot aimed at your feet results in a jam. Similarly, if you are facing a rushing forward player, aim the ball, so it bounces just beyond the reach of their backhand.

Dinking

When dinking, maintain your toes slightly below the line and remain compressed and forward-leaning. If you must enter the kitchen, consider stepping in with only one foot and then rapidly pushing off with this foot to return to your original position. You may need to make sideways modifications to stay connected to your partner. A side shuffle is a sideways stride movement (approximately a side-together-side footwork sequence). Maintain a square body to the ball position. Back up away from field shots aimed at your feet. Instead, reach inside the kitchen and return these shots.

A right-forehander's ground stroke should be performed with the left foot and left shoulder forward. The right foot and right shoulder are forward for a backhand groundstroke. However, you do not often have the opportunity to position yourself optimally.

Only Hit the Best Targets

The left-heel target is the essential target in Pickleball. Remember to turn left, left, and left. In general, the left-heel target for right-handed players is positioned to the left of the opponent's left heel. So, it's slightly to the left of being centered between your opponents, requiring the even-court opponent to attempt a low backhand shot.

A shot at this target is extremely tough to return, even when you are halted, squeezed, and leaning forward. A shot at this target produces a jam or causes you to run over the ball if you travel ahead. Even when dinking, this should be a primary aim until a quick volley game begins.

Maintain Your Paddle

The majority of striking occurs at close range among expert players. When you let go of your paddle, you become an easy, defenseless target for a fastball. When you're deep in the court, such as when returning a serve, keep the paddle up and in front of you with both hands on it.

When on the NVZ Line

Keep the paddle up (above your waist) and in front of you when completely up to the net, with the head of the paddle over your wrist. If the head of your paddle is below your wrist and a fastball strikes it, the impact will deflect the paddle face downward, leading the ball to likely fall into the net. If the paddle head is higher than your wrist, the deflection will drive the ball upward, likely sending it back across the net. Some instructors recommend keeping the paddle blade in a neutral position, perpendicular to the net. Other instructors recommend a slightly backhand or entirely backhand paddle stance for the at-the-line ready position. When the ball is pushed up, the paddle must rapidly move to a backhand position to enable a block or punch volley of the approaching fastball.

Many great players aid or guide their backhand backswing using their non-paddle hand. This is a fantastic concept. When both hands are on the paddle, your brain understands more precisely where it is, than when only one hand is on it.

Chapter Two

Why You Lose Points

You've probably heard that most rallies conclude with unforced errors, generally into the net, rather than dazzling victory shots. The primary root cause of many unforced mistakes is applying force when it should not be employed. To put it another way, players hit forcefully when they should hit lightly, and vice versa. This is particularly true for new and intermediate players. Hitting the ball harder diminishes control and increases mistakes, whereas hitting it gently promotes control and decreases errors.

The window you must hit through to be effective when hitting the ball hard from the serving line or any place deep on the court is quite narrow. You're in the net if you go too low. You're out-of-bounds if you get too high. When you hit the ball gently, the space you must hit across becomes much larger, and your chances of winning rise.

Let's look at some particular errors.

The Excessive Use of Power

The Serve

It makes no sense to employ a fast serving speed unless you have exceptional consistency with your serve. To serve deeper, strike the ball with a higher trajectory rather than a hard, flat trajectory. Because rallies are rarely won on a serve (even among elite players), most serious players should focus on serving consistency rather than serving speed.

The Return of Serve

The greatest error in power usage happens on the return of serve. A successful fastball return seldom results in anything, and a fastball return will punish you if you have inadequate mobility. When you use a fastball as a return of serve, it is quite tough to reach all the way to the NVZ line before the third shot comes back. It is far more vital to get to the NVZ line in time, than to make a fastball return of serve. A deep return is also preferable to a rapid return since the deep shot makes the key third shot more difficult. A slower arcing return will provide more depth, accuracy, and precision than a flat trajectory fastball return.

A floating backspin serve return is a terrific shot if you can execute and place it consistently because the spin makes the crucial third shot more difficult. Unless you can dependably put the shot in front of the intended opponent, employ a spin shot. As you progress to competition-level play, you should never miss a serve or a return of serve, and you should only give a short return of serve that invites a fastball on rare occasions.

The Third Shot

Likewise, among skilled 5.0-rated players, the bullet/block/drop approach is adopted in roughly 15% of third-shot scenarios, and only when the setting is excellent. The bullet third shot is not the finest option for a third shot. It's one of the worst since it can fall into the net or go out-of-bounds. A medium-speed, down-the-middle shot that bounces before, or at, your opponent's feet, on the other hand, produces the highest percentage of favorable rally results. A third shot that bounces before your opponent hits it is a greater percentage shot than one that can be volleyed back or one with a high fault rate, such as a lob or a fastball.

Hitting from Deep Against Good Net Players

When facing weak net players, hard hitters typically have the upper hand. If the net players are good, it's a different scenario. Fastball shots have a narrow window in which they can go over the net but not out-of-bounds. As a result, a significant portion will end up in the net. Another portion will be out-of-bounds, and strong players will be able to evaluate and avoid striking these. Most strong fastball shots will be dinked, blocked, or deflected back to you. A dink shot is an effective strategy to cope with a fastball from a deep player on the court.

You should be attempting to get there when you're not on the net. When your opponents are already at the net, chasing after sluggish shots is the greatest approach to gaining progress. So, if you're deep in the court and your opponents are at the net, it's better to target the kitchen with a slow, arcing drop shot if you have to hit up on the ball, which is nearly always the case. When facing net players, the basic rule of thumb is to hit up the ball lightly. You can strike forcefully when you can hit down on the ball, like with a smash. So, unless the ball is high, you should not be hitting fastballs to the team at the net from the far baseline portion of the court. You should instead be hitting slow, arcing drop shots.

Advanced Pickleball players, like advanced volleyball players, realize that scoring points from deep in the court will not win a match. A winning shot from deep on the court is uncommon. In doing so, you waste the rally by attempting low-percentage shots rather than harnessing the rally to make a high-percentage shot.

The Open-Court Put-Away Chance

This is your great chance. Your opponent is in hot water. They are wide off the court. They have popped the ball, providing you with an easy smash and a wide-open part of the court. Unfortunately, with what should be a "given," most intermediate players will make a mistake roughly one-third of the time. Don't utilize more power than required to make your unreachable put-away in an open-court setting.

The Underuse of Power

We've discussed the overuse of power; where does the underuse of power occur? The majority of high-powered action comes at the net if someone allows the ball to get too high. When starting or responding to the quick net play, you must beat reaction times with your initial shot, or risk losing the rally. So never try to start a fastball battle with a weak shot. Remember, among expert players, you should never throw a ball in the air to your opponent unless it's a deep lob shot, or a rapid shot aimed to beat their reaction time.

The skill of keeping the ball low and soft, regardless of how it is given to you, is an immensely useful skill. You may do this with a companion. Stand at the NVZ line while your practice partner opposite you hits you with various shots. All shots must be returned low and toward the kitchen. You may also use a practice wall like this. Alternate between hitting the ball strongly and softly, ensuring all soft shots go low and over the net.

Chapter Three

How to Practice Better

The Importance of Early Preparation Single-side singles. Divide the court in half along the middle line to create a rectangle ten feet wide by forty-four feet long. Play singles alone on this side of the court. This promotes the use of the third shot (drop shot) as well as the at-the-line style of play.

Preparing begins before you get onto the Pickleball court by ensuring you have everything you need. Although no one likes to have to leave the Pickleball courts early because they forgot or didn't have a certain item with them for their game, this is especially true when playing competitively. When competing in a Pickleball tournament, planning for, and preparing for a long day of Pickleball, and being at the Pickleball courts, is critical.

When getting ready to play Pickleball, you'll need a Pickleball paddle, a Pickleball, and correct Pickleball court shoes.

Not only should you be prepared before hitting the Pickleball courts, but you should also be prepared during each Pickleball point. To put it another way, be prepared on the Pickleball court!

The proper ready position on the Pickleball court is one of the most important concepts in Pickleball that is not taught or discussed enough. This is especially important when you are at the NVZ or kitchen line, or transitioning up the Pickleball court and entering the "no-man's" or "no-land" or the "transition area."

This ready posture consists of the following elements:

- The feet should be shoulder-width apart.
- With your knees bent and your weight on the balls of your feet, compress your body.
- Paddle with your paddle towards 10 or 11 o'clock if you're standing on a clock face (or 2 or 1 o'clock if you're a lefty)—as you should be in a semi-backhand position, your opponent should be able to read the face of your paddle. Keeping your paddle in this posture reduces your reaction time since you'll be near the net and your opponent more often when the Pickleball is thrown at you. Consequently, this semi-backhand stance allows you to respond faster to shots while still allowing you to flip your paddle and play a forehand. However, don't over-rotate to the 9 o'clock position (or 3 o'clock if you're a

lefty) since you'll be too focused on backhands. Maintain your paddle face at the 10 or 11 o'clock position (or 2 or 1 o'clock position if you're a lefty).

- Paddle forward with your paddle head up.

Reduce Unforced Errors

In the sport of Pickleball, like other sports, we all want to learn the secret ingredient, or the sophisticated spin technique, or the power striking and smashing, that doing so will take you to a win. What successful teams do most of the time isn't anything fancy or mysterious if you pay attention during league matches, or any other match. 70% of the time, successful teams make fewer unforced errors.

An unforced error occurs when a ball is hit directly to the person, and he/she has an easy chance to do anything they want in the return hit since they do not have to move much, lean, reach, or do anything else to hit the return, and the individual smacks the ball into the net or smashes it out.

At a lesser level of play, unforced errors at the 4.0+-level may be termed forced errors. A 4.0–5.0

level player can adequately manage a hit to them with considerable pace, spin, and even requiring a significant arm extension as an "easy" return. However, that same sort of shot coming at a 3 .0–3.5 level player would not be regarded as a potential for an unforced error (if hit out or into the net) since the ball is not an "easy" return hit at this level of play.

It's actually that easy. Minimize your unforced errors, and you have a higher chance of winning.

Furthermore, when focusing on better-talented players, 4.0–5.0, 28%–40% of total points earned come from unforced errors. Based on the data from these higher-level players, at least 50% or more of points earned in lower-level play are from unforced errors. Our own mistakes account for as much as half of the points we score in a game! Making it even more crucial in our leisure leagues and Pickleball communities that limiting our unforced errors is essential to success.

Generally, keeping the ball in play is your best buddy when playing Pickleball. One way to improve your shots of winning a game is to improve your team's efficiency in moving the ball over the net and into play. Make unforced errors and let the other team beat you instead of winning the game for yourself.

Forget about whaling on the ball with power shots that fly out, and don't attempt to force creative spin shots that go in or set up for slams. Also, don't aim for the line, which invariably hits just beyond the line and travels out. You are only defeating your squad by producing unforced errors. Instead, work on being calm and steady while maintaining control of the ball. Let your opponent's commit unforced errors by getting the ball over the net and into their court. You will win many matches whenever you commit fewer unforced errors than your rivals!

Begin examining your own play and checking in with yourself to identify instances in which you are making unforced errors.

Ways to Improve Your Pickleball Technique

Obtaining excellence typically necessitates receiving excellent coaching and instruction. You also need concentrated, goal-oriented practice and drills to refine your abilities and shots. A ball machine is a useful instrument for this. You also need to monitor and analyze gaps and progress. Video analysis and statistics are examples of tools. Finally, the coach must make modifications depending on the outcomes and remaining gaps.

The development process is often a continuous cycle of the following:

1. Teaching what to do
2. Practice
3. Evaluation/gap assessment
4. Corrections
5. Cycle repetition.

Despite how obvious all of this is, most players do not follow it. As a result, they only produce modest advances, if any at all.

Get Instruction/Expert Assistance

Almost every outstanding athlete in every sport had a coach. A qualified coach can likely identify and correct your most serious flaws in just a few hours. A coach may assist you in avoiding the trial-and-error process and avoiding rookie mistakes so that you can rapidly get to the point of doing things correctly. You may have to study books, watch videos, and seek guidance from the top players in your region if you don't have a coach.

Practice/Drills

You must put your coach's instructions into practice. Practice time will improve players at all levels more than playing time. Almost all sports follow this guideline. Pros spend their valuable time practicing shots and exercises rather than playing games. You must repeat the same shot to enhance shot-making abilities in tennis, golf, or Pickleball.

The following are some of the most significant drills and most can be done with a partner:

- The third shot drill (drop shot). This is the most crucial and challenging ability you need to master Pickleball.

- Practice your dinking. You must learn to direct the ball and keep it low in order to prevent flubs.

- An approaching fastball dinked. You might play with a partner or a ball machine.

Learn to dink an approaching fastball or produce an angled dink.

- Overhead fake smash/dink. You might play with a partner or a ball machine. Fake a smash by doing an overhead dink instead.

- Surprising offensive lobs. You must practice the necessary deception and touch to get a trajectory that is high enough without being too short or too lengthy.

- Judging out-balls. You might play with a partner or a ball machine. You must perfect the calibration that prevents you from hitting out-balls.

- Fast-game practice. This works best with four people. If you have one partner, begin with dinking back and forth with your partner, utilizing only half of the court. Each time you start and win a fastball fight, you get the point. Each time you start and lose a fastball fight, you lose a point. You will quickly learn when to, and when not to start a fight.

Chapter Four

The Dos and Don'ts of Hitting Technique

The Importance of Hitting Technique

It goes against our natural tendency to get out of the path of a ball that is easily attainable, possibly a ball below the level of our head. Unless instructed to the contrary, most players will attempt to hit every shot they can reach. As a result, most players will hit numerous balls that would otherwise be out-of-bounds. It appears that avoiding striking a ball that then landed inbounds would be quite detrimental. The difficulty is that this no-chance technique implies that ten or more balls that were heading out-of-bounds were maintained in play. Of course, every advantage counts among rivals, and you can't afford to waste chances to win a rally.

Professional rivals are obsessed with not hitting out-balls, and they should be because several points are at risk on this single problem. Approximately half of the Pickleball rallies go through all four phases, culminating in quick-volley action. These fastball rallies rapidly get sloppy. The ball is almost out-of-bounds by the third or fourth hit. You can't hit these out-balls when your opponents are cleverly dodging them and expect to win the match.

Follow these strategies to make yourself into a wise player when it comes to not hitting out-balls:

- Understand your position on the court. Beginners frequently volley back out-balls while standing on or near the baseline. So, pay attention to ball speed and height, as well as your position on the court.

- Get yourself adjusted. You must develop an understanding of the speeds and trajectories that lead to a ball going out-of-bounds. Begin with this rule: while you are in the NVZ, any fastball that is shoulder height or above will most likely go out-of-bounds. So, to begin, get out of the way of any swift shot at shoulder height or above and then observe the effects. You'll almost probably be correct the majority of the time. Then, reduce the maximum permissible height to sternum level and see the consequences. You'll still be correct most of the time with fastballs. Of course, ball speed and trajectory will both influence which shots are successful and which are not. The idea is to calibrate yourself and enhance your ability to judge out-balls.

- Recognize the speed early. Observing your opponent as they prepare to bat is the greatest technique to predict if a fastball will be thrown. A windup (shoulder turn and extended backswing) indicates a fastball. When you notice a windup, go into out-ball-assessment mode right away. Good players will strive to conceal their fastball strategy. However, keep an eye on the paddle speed to indicate the ball speed early. Good players will be able to predict the ball's speed before it is hit.

- Adjust your calibration as needed. It's difficult to admit, but you need to modify your calibration so that some shots you're dodging stay within the borders.

- Understand which paths do not work. If your opponent attempts a slap shot (a shot to the body) off a low dink bounce or a dink bounce far inside the kitchen, dodge it as soon as you notice fastball intent. These shots almost always fall out-of-bounds. When your opponent attempts to get aggressive with a ball lower than the net's height, the ball is likely to go out-of-bounds. A midcourt ground stroke explosion that is more than a foot above the net is out-of-bounds.

- Follow your calibration. Your calibration may not be exact, but you must abide by it by staying out of the way of any shots that appear to be going out. You must keep an eye on the outcomes. Are the majority of the deflected shots going out-of-bounds? Your objective should be to have made the right judgments most of the time but not always. You're still hitting too many out-balls if all the shots you avoided go out-of-bounds.

By the way, this is a situation where a ball machine would be really useful. Set the ball speed to high and pick an angle for the machine that delivers balls eighteen inches out-of-bounds from a midcourt machine placement. Find another angle that keeps the balls in play. Alternate between the two views as you fire shots from the machine to a human at the NVZ line. The student should make rapid progress in judging in-and-out-balls.

Whereas novice players would constantly aim to hit rather than take chances, expert players will often opt not to hit and accept that they will be correct most of the time. This is a high-probability play.

When watching a professional-level play, like the Minto US Open Pro Division Gold Medal Match, you'll see that the pros dodge shots that end up extremely near the baseline, with some remaining within boundaries. The fact that some shots stayed inbounds does not indicate that they are having difficulty with this aspect of their game. Instead, it indicates that this aspect of their game is most likely optimized.

Dodging out-balls is also an important approach when facing bangers or really hard hitters. Instead of drop shots, several players employ strong hits or fastballs as third shots. Hard hitters do well against opponents who save and return their out-balls, but they are disadvantaged by opponents who can predict when such shots are heading out-of-bounds.

Why Doesn't the Ball Go Where You Aim?

A common misunderstanding among Pickleball players is that hitting a certain place on the court is more difficult than they think it is. Most individuals believe the ball should move in the direction their paddle aims. However, this is not always the case. Yes, it is an infuriating truth that the ball does not always move following the route of the strike. In other words, the ball does not travel where the paddle is directed.

Consider a basic example: a crosscourt shot is coming toward you, and you just want to stop it. So, you point your paddle straight ahead. Does the ball move ahead perpendicular to your paddle's face? No. Instead, it exits the paddle at the same angle from which it entered. It's known as the “law of reflection” in physics.

Here's another example: you're completely forward at the NVZ line when your extremely deep opponent strikes you with a fastball. You want to dink (block) it toward the sideline. You can't aim the paddle directly at the goal in this instance. Instead, aim it gently toward the direction from which the ball is coming.

To complicate the situation, ball spin can raise the angle of reflection even more, causing the ball to come off the paddle at an angle that is far from where you want it.

Now consider the standard case: a shot is coming at you from an unexpected direction, and you are directing your paddle at a target and striking the ball. Will the ball land on the target? Almost definitely not. The paddle's forward motion lessens but does not eliminate the angle of reflection.

The narrower the angle of reflection, the faster the paddle goes into the ball. In other words, a rapid strike will cause the ball to come off the paddle closer to the direction the paddle is targeted.

Please don't take this to indicate that striking harder is always better.

Important Points:

1. It will be simpler to control the ball's direction if the return does not modify the ball angle, i.e., if the ball is sent back in the same direction it arrived. At contact, the incoming and outgoing directions of the ball are the same and perpendicular to the face of the paddle. As a result, both the angle of incidence and the angle of reflection are zero. Unless the ball has spin, it will go in the direction of the paddle path, whether the player swings forcefully, softly, or any-

where between. While simple to execute, such shots are not always the best option.

2. Use caution when attempting to shift the direction of the ball. You must account for the angle of reflection while changing the ball's direction. This is done as follows: if the ball is coming from the crosscourt side and you want to send it straight ahead, perpendicular to the net, your swing path and paddle face must be slightly crosscourt, that is, slightly toward the direction the ball is coming from. The amount of compensation will be determined by how hard you hit. You can't play superb Pickleball unless you can adjust the ball's direction. A terrific wall practice drill is to stand in a corner and hit each wall alternately.

3. Make room for mistakes. The further you are from the net, the more crucial it is to avoid the sidelines. Aside from the angle of reflection issue, there is the spin issue. It's difficult to predict the direction and degree of ball spin. If you're at your baseline, and there's no spin or intentional ball direction adjustment, a five-degree paddle face mistake equates to being four feet off-target at

your opponent's end of the court. So, leave room for the mistake!

Here are Some Examples of Frequent Errors

When you change the ball's direction and attempt a delicate shot like a dink, the angle of reflection is huge, and you can easily run wide and out-of-bounds. This is a frequent rookie error. It's far easier and safer to take a gentle shot and modify its direction to a longer, quicker shot than the opposite.

Miscellaneous Shots and Situations

High Bounce Close to the Net

A high, defensive lob is quite brief. It appears like it will not make it over the net, yet it does. How do you deal with this? Of course, you can't strike it till after the bounce since it's in the kitchen. The ball will be approximately 36 inches in height after the bounce. If your opponents are within ten feet of the ball, a little disguised dink to put the ball just barely back across the net should be a victory.

But suppose your opponents are all in. If the ball comes up higher than the net, you might try a body shot to a close opponent. However, given the ball is close to the net and would most likely come up somewhat above it, opt to smash a steeply slanted (and quite sharply down) shot to send the ball across and wide.

If the high shot appears certain to cross the net and you're close to a sideline, attempt the Erne shot described below.

Erne's Shot

You are dinking back and forth with your opponent along a sideline. You can see that they will stay on the sidelines. You can move to the side of the court (outside the court), close to the net, and post to smash the ball as it passes through. When heading to the side area, most players attempt to avoid walking into the kitchen. If you contact the NVZ for any reason, you cannot volley the return until both feet are entirely beyond the NVZ.

Follow-through lets your paddle break the net plane but not contact it. You can even walk around the net post and cross the net's imaginary extension as long as you don't touch the opponent's court. To set up the Erne shot, you may occasionally entice your opponent into hitting it to you along the sideline. If your opponent is a little too close to the center for you to get the ball past them along the sideline, they will most likely only be able to return the ball forward, not crosscourt. Outside the dinking game, you can employ the Erne shot if an opponent hits a third shot (drop shot) that is too close to a sideline or if a short lob comes close to a sideline.

Around the Post

You're dinking when a sharply slanted shot sends you wide, outside the court. Only your partner remains to cover the entire court. The worst thing you can do is hit the ball to a close opponent. Going straight across the court and into the kitchen is a better idea. If the ball is wide, though, the around-the-post shot gives you the highest chance of winning. You should practice this shot with drills ahead of time to have the talent and presence of mind to use it when the moment arises. Wait until the ball almost bounces a second time (almost reaches the ground) before striking it to make it feasible to acquire the largest width (distance beyond the post). Then hit low and into the opposing team's court. It should be noted that the ball does not have to cross the net again. And the return might be much lower than the net's height, for example, just barely above the ground.

The Keep-Them-Back Shot

After your third shot (a drop shot) landed in the kitchen, you are now on your way to the NVZ line. When the keep-them-back shot comes your way, you're still five or six feet from the NVZ line. This shot is low and comes to your forehand, yet it may be volleyed. What are you going to do? A cautious shot would be to play a drop shot into the kitchen and then move toward the NVZ line. However, this is an excellent opportunity to throw a fastball to the soft middle (the region between your two opponents), which usually results in a weak or popped-up return.

Player in the Kitchen

Your shot strikes the top of the net but dribbles over it into the kitchen area of your close opponent. They get the ball back over the net to you but are unable to leave the kitchen. What are you going to do? Send the ball back to them, trying a body shot, unless they are really quick in getting back behind the NVZ line.

Once your opponent goes inside the kitchen with both feet, they must return both feet to the ground outside of the kitchen (beyond the NVZ line) before making a volley shot. This is a difficult task. It's also worth noting that if this happens to you, you should return the shot crosscourt to allow time to go back behind the line (and make a body shot attempt more difficult). Remember that you should not place both feet in the kitchen unless absolutely necessary.

Fake Poach and Open Net Position/Poach

Your teammate was dragged off the court by a spectacular crosscourt dink to the sideline, and they are unable to recover in time to field the following shot. Unfortunately, they did not lob but instead struck the ball at a nearby opponent. As a result, their net position is exposed, and you must defend the entire court. What are you going to do? This is an extremely tough position to manage. Staying in place, protecting your section of the court, is the worst thing you can do. Moving to the center of the court is a somewhat better option. This allows you to take a passing shot through your teammate's open floor side. To correctly bisect your opponent's opportunity angle, you must advance slightly into your teammate's unoccupied court. The opponent will be more likely to hit in this direction rather than crosscourt. You may also do a faux poach when you have an open net position. The false poach may lure the shot directly to you.

Overcome the Defensive Wall

So long as the ball bounces between hits, the defensive wall has plenty of time to glide back and forth. If you receive a volleyed shot near the sideline, a fast crosscourt dink may be able to outrace your distant opponent for a winner or weak return.

Angled Semi-Smash Put-Away Shot

You are given an air ball (one that may be volleyed) slightly higher than the net's height. Your opponents have not yet completely advanced. What are you going to do? Of course, you could play a keep-them-back shot aimed at the left heel. However, if you hit a hard crosscourt with as much speed as possible, you are more likely to obtain a winner. This should render the ball inaccessible.

Chapter Five

The Right Hit at the Right Time

Shots to Avoid

Mostly all Pickleball players undervalue the difficulty of hitting a target area on the court. As a result, there is little room for mistakes, including out-of-bounds shots. Try this assessment to better persuade yourself of the difficulties of ball placement. Attempt to return all serves for the game's duration to the intended spot, which should necessitate a backhand return for a right-handed player.

Certain shots should be avoided. Here are several shots to avoid.

Lobbing from the Baseline or Deep in the Court

Lobbing from the baseline is acceptable when you are in difficulties, such as when a net man smashes a ball at you. Lobbing from the baseline while you're not in difficulty, on the other hand, is typically a bad idea. It's tempting to go over the heads of the net crew, especially as a third shot. Sneaky lobs while dinking are successful, but lobs from the baseline or deep in the court are low-percentage shots since your opponents have ample time to react and move. If you're strong at lobbing, you could do well against guys with limited mobility or players who miss their smash shots. However, against skilled players, you will almost certainly lose two points for every point earned. If you're not very good at lobbing, you'll hit half of your lobs too short, resulting in a smash, and half too long, resulting in out-of-bounds. A better option is to concentrate on getting to the net by pursuing a gentle shot meant to drop into the NVZ.

Long Crosscourt Shots toward a Sideline

It's fine to hit diagonally from the NVZ line toward a kitchen sideline, like when dinking. Clearing the middle for a down-the-center victory is an excellent tactic. A crosscourt drop shot intended to land in the kitchen is likewise acceptable. On the other hand, a long crosscourt shot toward the sideline from the baseline or from deep in the court is a low-percentage shot. Again, publications on doubles tennis strategy advise against these shots since they frequently end in out-of-bounds situations. A top-tier player will rarely try such a long diagonal shot.

Going Down the Sideline When You Are Deep

You're deep in the court, and it looks like your near opponent at the NVZ line has left the sideline alley unguarded. It would be a thrill to scorch this man and smoke a fastball down the right field line! When you succeed in making such a shot, you feel enormous pride. It's the equivalent of making a 25-foot jump shot. You go for it, believing no guts, no glory. Unfortunately, your shot misses the mark. Was the miss unintentional?

No. Such a shot has a strong chance of being picked off by the near-net player or sailing wide out-of-bounds. A 5.0-rated player is unlikely to attempt such a down-the-sideline shot. A better option is to concentrate on getting to the net by placing a drop shot into the kitchen. Only drive along the sideline if the hole is large enough to accommodate a vehicle.

If your near opponent is too far to the center, hitting along the sideline from the NVZ line or close to the NVZ line might be a superb shot, especially if they are also pushing forward. Also, if a volley chance presents itself at the NVZ line, this may be a nice time to go down the line, especially if the shot causes a reach-out or a paddle flip, say, from backhand to forehand.

Deep in the Court Topspin Fastball Shots

In doubles Pickleball, fastball ground-stroke shots are seldom required. However, in the odd scenario of a deep player hitting another deep player, such a shot is used to make the third shot drive. Fastball shots sent from deep in the court have a 25% direct failure rate among mid-level players, either going into the net or out-of-bounds deep. The addition of a topspin increases the difficulty of the shot. Unlike table tennis, topspin cannot be added by coming over the top of the ball. You must instead provide lift by touching the ball below the center as the paddle scrapes upward.

Most low-percentage shots result from impatience, desperation, or the beginner's desire to win every shot. You just cannot aim for victory with every shot. Instead, you must patiently wait for an opening, or create conditions that will allow you to win.

Chapter Six

The Winning Strategy

To win at Pickleball, you must have skills, movement, and strategy. You need to have ball-striking and shot-making abilities, the ability to move fast to field shots, and complete awareness of strategy—where to be, and where to strike the ball in every circumstance.

It's not just what you know that makes you stand out; it's how you think that does. Many of the world's top athletes in sports like golf, tennis, soccer, and basketball believe that it is not a person's skill set that distinguishes the excellent from the great. But it's more about how elite players think. How they win is what matters. It's how they do things. It's all about execution. In other words, they have a long-term view and often consider many shots ahead, rather than simply reacting. Pickleball is a fantastic example of this; the finest players are distinguished from the others by the gap in their mentality.

Rookies don't play with a plan. Their response is one of reaction. They're going all-out to win the rally. So, they try for a quick serve, a fast return of serve... a fast every shot. A soft shot intended to land in the kitchen is nearly always the first shot after the return of serve in advanced play. A similar rookie player in volleyball would strive to hit a winner from deep in the court rather than laboring to build up a spike.

The intermediate player may realize the significance of moving completely forward immediately, but they will still try to accomplish too much, too quickly. An intermediate player will take a dangerous shot as soon as they get up to the line.

The 5.0-rated player understands that attempting to win the rally before putting all their energy into it is rarely a good idea. Once at the NVZ line, the 5.0-rated player understands it's better to bide your time in a dinking exchange and wait patiently for a good chance, before making an aggressive move.

Rally length and hit count data bear this out. Most rallies in novice play are decided in five shots or less. Of course, some of these rallies finish quickly owing to flubs and mishits. Poor planning, on the other hand, is also a factor. On average, rallies with a skill level of 3.5–4.0 last longer and feature more hits than novice rallies. Poor shot selection and planning often cause the demise of these rallies. Although you can see the talent and athleticism at this level, there is also a sense of restraint and a willingness to wait for the ideal chance to attack. Dinking exchanges may typically carry on for ten or more shots.

Recall the old phrase, "Never intervene with an opponent when he's in the process of destroying himself." Pickleball is a game that makes use of this regulation. Rather than taking chances with aggression, very often, the greatest technique is just to continue to return the ball to your opponent. Under such a tactic, a hasty or less-skilled opponent will likely be the first to a fault. Of course, this doesn't imply that you offer your opponent shots that provide an advantage.

Striving to do Too Much, Too Fast, and With a Bad Plan

Most notably, 4.0-level, and lower players overextend themselves while maintaining an inadequate setup. They attempt to accomplish too much with their serve and the return of serve. On the sidelines, they're getting too close. Too many angles are attempted, such as an acute turn or a turn to the sideline. They go for greater authority than is required. On keep-them-back shots, they go too deep. On smash shots, they go out-of-bounds by creating too steep an angle or too much depth. They begin the fastball battle with a ball that is too low. They dink the ball too deep, allowing their opponents to control it.

They try to lob rather than to continue dinking. When they lob, they go for too much depth. Finally, they are losing many rallies due to their too ambitious play. Playing with a partner who consistently makes mistakes due to attempting to accomplish too much is a stressful experience.

Begin with the following method, which is summarized as follows:

1. Priority number one while serving is to serve without making any errors. If you are having problems, strike slowly and aim towards the middle of the box.

2. When returning the serve, go for the opponent with the weakest third-shot skill. Return the serve with a semi-lob if required, so you are completely in place at the NVZ line on time, before the third shot comes over the net.

3. Thirdly, if your opponents are completely forward, utilize the drop shot into the kitchen for the third time to finish the shot. If they are not at the line as they should be, strike at the left-heel target of the deeper player. If your third shot is a bit high, you

may have to make a second or third drop shot effort to permit moving fully forward. Be patient and ignore the desire to smash the defense wall. Remember, if you have to hit up on the ball, hit softly.

4. Play the keep-them-back shot by staying completely forward, reaching in and volleying the shot back, and taking care not to offer the opponent a shot for another volley shot.

5. Continue to play keep-them-back shots going low to the deeper player's backhand if the third shot goes into the kitchen and your opponents are still not up to the NVZ line.

6. Once all players are fully forward, commit to being patient with the dinking procedure. Keep your body glued to the NVZ line and prevent unnecessarily backing up or moving your feet. Volley dink shots back, rather than backing up to let them bounce. Try to keep the dink shots headed to player's backhands. Stress your opponents, but remember that remaining on the point is more crucial than going for

a reckless winner. Don't throw a fastball if the ball is below the net's height. A suitable objective would be a spot that necessitates a reach-out or paddle flip if you desire to go quickly.

Getting your team fully ahead as early as possible and keeping the other team behind as long as possible is the basic Pickleball strategy, as you can probably understand right now. If you have to hit up on the ball, which is usually always, hit gentle shots meant to bounce before being returned. If all players go completely forward, keep the ball low and soft (dink it) until a put-away opportunity comes.

How to Handle the Power Player

Battle of the Bangers

For a variety of reasons, hard-hitting bangers fare well among mid-level players. Mid-level players are frequently absent from the net where they should be. This indicates that the fastball can hit the feet. Mid-level players are likewise baffled by an oncoming fastball (like dinking it or blocking it to the backhand). Mid-level players lack the ability to evaluate and consequently return out-balls. Furthermore, many mid-level players cannot manage the speed and consequently flub the fastball return. So, here's how to deal with abrasive opponents.

When You Serve

If you have the talent to do it consistently, consider serving to the banger's backhand since this should result in a worse serve return. Furthermore, when hitting the banger, attempt to keep the majority of your shots to the banger's backhand.

Return Serve

You're up against a banger with a lightning-fast serve. Make sure you're well back from the baseline and wait for the ball to fall before striking it. It is not necessary for your return-of-serve shot to be fast, but it is advantageous if it is deep. Assume you're up against two bangers who will both hit third fastball strikes. Either strike the weaker banger or the banger's left-heel target on the even court.

When You Are Fielding the Third Shot

When playing against bangers, getting to the NVZ line in time for the third shot is even more important. If you take your time moving forward, you invite a fastball shot to halt your progress. So, you're at the NVZ line, and the banger is shooting at you. It's critical to be able to gauge and not hit out-balls in this case. A large majority of fastball third-pitch attempts will be out-of-bounds.

Dink the fastball shot if the banger is deep (close to, or beyond the baseline). In addition, all players must learn how to dink back approaching fastball pitches. As a final option, just block the shot at the left heel target, attempting to halt forward movement. Remember to keep them back when they return.

The Fourth Shot and Beyond

Again, while hitting a banger, aim to keep the majority of your shots to the banger's backhand and left heel. When your opponent attempts to get aggressive with a ball lower than the net's height, the shot almost always goes out-of-bounds.

Drills

You must be able to handle fastballs to be a competent Pickleball player. This is something that a practice partner can assist you with. Start by standing at the NVZ line and allowing the fastball to come to you from deep. Learn to block fastballs at the sender's feet and to dink them into the kitchen and toward the sideline. Allow fastballs to come to you from a closer distance as you improve.

Hitting volley shots on a backboard is an excellent approach to improve reflexes and the ability to manage quick strokes. Practice volleying continuously without letting the ball bounce. Increase your striking speed and distance from the wall as you go.

Developing the Third Shot

The third shot, a soft drop shot into the kitchen, is used by the best players more than seventy-five percent of the time. The best way you can improve your game—if you want to join the ranks of good players—is to concentrate on making drop shots into the kitchen. The quicker you figure out how to achieve this, the better. You employ this drop shot for the third shot, and if you need to hit up on the ball and have two opponents at the net. One of the key differences between the 5.0-, 4.5-, and 4.0-rated players is their ability with the third shot (drop shot). As previously stated in this book, when the serving team makes the third shot of the game (the return of the return-of-serve) from deep in the court against net players, this shot alone has a 17% chance of explicitly inflicting the serving team to lose the rally, usually by the ball going into the net or being smashed back. The 17% figure comes from a study of top 5.0-level players. For 4.5-level players, the figure rises to 27%.

The Most Effective Method

Before we get into drills, let's learn how to set up and hit the ball. Consistency in setup is one of the keys to shot consistency. In golf, there is an analog with the chip shot. To get consistent distance, you must have a consistent setup, swing, and swing speed, as well as make excellent contact with the ball.

Here are some ideas:

- Make a good stroke with the ball. Don't poke, punch, or flick your wrist at it. Instead, employ a backswing, a straight line through the contact zone, and a follow-through into the target, rising slightly forward into the stroke. After the strike, top players will use their forward momentum for rushing forward. Use a linear "blocking" stroke for forehand third shots, with the paddle face directed upward. Do the same on third backhand shots, aiming the paddle face ahead of the strike.

- Maintain your position behind the baseline until you can determine the depth of the service return shot. A beginner's error is to move too rapidly forward, needing a backward movement to field a serve return shot. Moving backward makes it tough to produce a solid third shot (drop shot). Instead, you should be moving forward into a strike.

- Move fast to the ball so that you have both feet in position and are properly placed before striking the ball. When you're moving or reaching for the ball, it's tough to produce a decent third shot.

- Position yourself to get the most out of your forehand hits. Some players can create excellent third shots with their backhand. Many players, in fact, prefer to make the shot with their backhand. Most players, though, will achieve more consistency with forehand strokes. So, when receiving the return of serve, stand to the left of the middle of the box to maximize forehand strokes (for a right-handed player).

- Scoop up the ball as it is falling and strike it from beneath. That reduces the effect of service return backspin and lets you use a more consistent paddle angle for all third shots. You can't always get into the position you want with some serve returns.

Drill with a Partner

This simple exercise can be done with a practice partner to help you refine this shot. Begin by dinking back and forth with your practice partner up to the NVZ line. Slowly advance closer to the court while maintaining your practice partner at the line. Continue to try to drop shots into the kitchen as you move away from it, and finally to the baseline. The arcing trajectory is necessary for this shot's perfection. As the ball crosses the net, you will see that it drops. The trajectory's peak is directly in front of the net. Shots that go a bit too high are preferable to shots that go into the net.

Wall Drill

To practice this shot, utilize a backboard wall drill. If the wall is not designated to indicate a net, use a strip of painter's tape at net height to approximate the top of the net tape. Place yourself around 22-feet away from the wall. First, strike the ball hard and high into the wall so that the return bounce returns the ball back to you (twenty-two feet from the wall). Next, attempt a drop shot, so the ball lowers as it hits the wall. Make an attempt to strike the wall one to two feet above the tape. When the ball returns to you, it will bounce two or three times before returning to your place. To repeat the pattern, strike the ball high and hard at the wall after its second or third bounce. You may only practice the drop shot every other time.

Ball Toss Drill

Put aside your paddle, stand near the baseline, and aim to land the ball in the kitchen to get a feel for the speed and trajectory necessary for the third shot. Repeat until you acquire a sense of the required speed and trajectory. Now grab your paddle and hit the ball into the kitchen with a similar trajectory.

Short/ Deep Strategies

Most of the placement options presented so far have focused on the left-to-right or horizontal placement, rather than depth placement. Now we'll discuss delivering short shots to deep players, and deep shots or lobs to net players.

When Should You Lob?

Offensive Lobs

Well-disguised offensive lobs sent from near the NVZ line against opponents who are also at the NVZ line have the highest probability of success.

This lob shot is great when your opponent is moving forward or just stepping out of the kitchen. Here are some offensive lob strategies:

1. Drive your opponent into the kitchen with a short dink, followed by a lob over their head.
2. Another good opportunity for an offensive lob is when the ball reaches the net on your side. Of course, if the ball topples over, it will remain extremely close to the net.
3.

Here's another situation where an attacking lob might be effective. You're in the middle of the court, hitting an opponent at the net. Instead of returning the shot to you to keep you deep, your opponent dinks the ball, pushing you to scramble forward. You just need to get to the ball before momentum sweeps it into the kitchen. This is an excellent opportunity for an attacking lob.

4. You're in the odd court, having a dinking exchange. Your opponent makes a powerful crosscourt shot, knocking you off the court. A quick crosscourt return towards the kitchen would be an excellent reaction. But imagine you are unable to make such a shot. A crosscourt lob to the far back corner (over your near opponent's left shoulder) might be an option.

5. You face a right-handed opponent on the even court and a left-handed player on the odd court. As a result, both backhands are in the middle. This is an excellent setup for a lob down the center.

The element of surprise is essential when it comes to attacking lobs. So, until the very last second, make the shot look like a dink. The safest ball path is over the left shoulder of a right-handed player, over the right shoulder of a left-handed player, or down the center line.

Anyone who enjoys throwing offensive lobs should strive to keep track of their success/failure rates. Continue lobbing if your triumphs outnumber your failures.

Many Pickleball coaches advise against employing offensive lobs, pointing out that the pros seldom use them, and that most ordinary players lose more rallies trying to utilize them than they win. Indeed, most players believe they have greater success with their lobs than they actually do. It's aggravating to play with a partner who consistently throws terrible lobs. So, ensure you base your decision on the success/failure facts.

The Defensive Lob

This is normally a last resort shot. Tennis players have an old saying: "When in deep difficulty, lob over the center of the tape." Yes, this also applies to Pickleball. The lob buys you time to reposition yourself. Suppose you can effectively perform a deep lob while you are in trouble. In that case, you may quickly move from being in trouble to being in a better position, especially if your opponent allows the long lob to bounce before striking. A crisp crosscourt shot into the kitchen, against a lob if you are near the net and in difficulties, possibly dragged out too wide.

What to Do After Hitting a Lob

You or your teammate made a lob shot. What should you do now?

- If the lob is short and your opponent is going to smash it, grab as much back as you can while remaining compact and ready.
- If the lob is deep, but your opponent is likely to smash it, go as far forward as possible near the NVZ line.
- If the lob is deep and your opponent will let the shot bounce, go all the way forward to the NVZ line.

Wind Considerations

Most experienced lobbers like to lob into a slight breeze when playing outside. This appears to be paradoxical. When lobbing, however, striking against the wind blunts the trajectory, aids in keeping the ball inbounds, and produces a wonderful upside-down U-shaped trajectory that brings the ball down in a near-vertical course. Similarly, most lobbers dislike the tailwind lob's trajectory and out-of-bounds risk. Of course, you should avoid lobbing in high and violent winds.

How to Deal with Offensive Lobs—Lobs from the NVZ Line over Net Players

The best defense against an attacking lob is to be on the lookout for it.

If you can read over-your-head offensive lobs given by your close opponent a second ahead of time, you can take a few rapid steps back and jump to reach it. If you can't get to it, it's probably out-of-bounds. If you notice it coming and react fast, it's impossible to lob over your head.

Assume this lob flies over your head, and you are unable to catch it. Get the lobs that go over your partner's head and vice versa. Most social and recreational players cannot track down a lob that has gone over their heads. In other words, if they don't catch the lob before it passes them, they won't be able to collect it afterward. So, in social play, fielding the lob that passes over your partner should become second nature for both players. Every lob requires quick and dependable communication.

When fielding a lob, you should strive to get into position as fast as possible to prevent being struck while drifting backward or rushing. If you are quite certain that the lob will be inbounds, or if your partner exclaims that it is, attempt to play the lob with a smash if feasible.

Allow the ball to bounce if the lob will land near the line. After the bounce, aim to make as much progress ahead as possible by hitting a drop shot into the kitchen.

How to Deal with Defensive Lobs

Most defensive lobs, especially those coming from the opponent's baseline, should give you plenty of time to get into position. Your partner should assess the trajectory and remark, "bounce it" or "good." As previously said, if you are very certain, the lob will be inbounds, or if your teammate exclaims that it is, play the lob with a smash if feasible. Allow the ball to bounce if the lob will land near the line. After the bounce, aim to make as much progress ahead as possible by hitting a drop shot into the kitchen. Having the ball bounce just inbounds obviously puts you at a significant disadvantage to your opponents because you will have to restart your trek to the NVZ line.

What to Do When You Are Deep

You've just been pulled past the baseline as far as possible after receiving a fantastic, deep, topspin lob shot. Your opponents have strategically placed themselves along the NVZ line. What are you going to do?

First Choice

Making a drop shot into the kitchen from this far back would be challenging, but it would be your first option. Err on the side of too deep (your shot gets volleyed back) rather than not deep enough (into the net). Follow the shot and make as much forward progress as you can.

In general, partners should play alongside, or even with one another. However, this regulation does not apply when a player is dragged beyond the baseline, as when fielding a deep lob. If you are pulled beyond the baseline, your partner should move forward significantly to field a possible dink back of your lob return shot. If the lob return shot brings up a smash from the NVZ line, the lobber and partner must go behind the baseline to field the smash.

Second Choice

If you field a deep lob, your next option for a return shot is a lob to the middle of the non-kitchen area, erring on the side of too shallow rather than too deep (out-of-bounds). A smash will occur if the lob is too shallow, so keep back to cope with this. If you must hit a fastball, go crosscourt to offer your partner a greater opportunity of fielding a dink-back of your stroke.

Lobs are an excellent illustration of how some shots perform well in certain situations but not in others. Outdoor play allows for less ball control. On the other hand, lobs are often and successfully used in indoor play against less mobile opponents.

Lobbing ability is especially vital for indoor players. Simply lob the ball back and forth with a partner, attempting to land the ball in the back half of the service courts.

Three Great Short Shots to Master

Hitting short shots against fast, mobile opponents deep in the court is typically a mistake since you give them a quick and simple path to the net. The usual norm is to keep them back when they return. Short shots, on the other hand, might be effective against your ordinary, slow opponent.

1. **The Overhead Smash Fake (Overhead Dink):** the overhead smash fake (overhead dink) is an excellent shot to perfect. While it will not work against speedy opponents, it will work against the majority of them. The shot seems to be a smash until you halt your paddle at the last second, allowing the ball to bounce off your paddle and fall over the net. Use this stroke when both of your opponents are deep on the court and expecting a smash.

   a. **Here's an example:** the third shot from your opponent was high. You send it back to their left heel with as much force as you can muster. Now that your opponent is in jeopardy, he tosses over a poor defensive lob. Both opponents are standing just behind the baseline, waiting for a smash. You set up and stance for a smash, then deliver the overhead dink. You'll probably discover that your success rate with this shot is higher than your success rate with a smash. Many player's smashes either fail to produce a winner or go into the goal or out-of-bounds. You may practice this shot by standing against a towering wall. Direct the ball high up on the wall so that it rebounds off the wall even higher, giving you a chance to practice fake smash.

2. **Angle Dink of Incoming Fastball:** when your opponents are deep and hit a fastball to you at the NVZ line, a smart technique is to dink the ball or dink it toward the deepest opponent's sideline. It's tough to decelerate a shot, but being able to dink back a fastball is a valuable talent. You may improve your shot by practicing with a partner or a ball machine.

3. **Angle Dink of an Incoming Third Shot from Deep:** keep in mind that this will only work against opponents with limited mobility. Assume you hit a terrific semi-lob return of serve that landed on, or near the baseline. Your opponent attempts a third shot (drop shot) into the kitchen, a difficult shot from deep. Their shot is a touch high, allowing you to reach into the

kitchen and volley it. As you begin to hit the ball, your opponent comes to a halt and does a split-step. Normally, you'd play a keep-them-back shot, aiming for the left heel. However, in the scenario mentioned, your opponent should be very far back because they were initially deep and then halted because their shot may be volleyed. If this opponent has limited mobility, a dink toward their sideline (away from their partner but not too close to the sideline) might be a winning play.

Chapter Seven

Advanced Strategies

Stroke Techniques

Take a look at these exciting and risky, yet really successful advanced shots. Keep in mind that these shots should only be used as tactics and not as regular shots. However, when the chance presents itself, these shots may be lethal.

The Dink Fake

This is one of the most cunning and deceptive shots in Pickleball. The dink fake is devastating if done right, but it's tough to pull off.

The dink fake is when you pretend to be ready to dink a semi-high ball but end up driving it instead. It's quick and may be utilized as a third-shot drive if the return is short.

There are two conditions for this shot to be successful:

1. You must have enough topspin.

2. The ball must be high enough.

The ball must be high enough for this shot, or it will just fall into the net. On the other hand, you must apply enough topspin so that it bends over the net and does not go out of the baseline.

It's time to dust up your acting abilities. Convince your opponent to believe you're about to dink the ball, then drive it all at once. The idea here is to make it appear out of nowhere. You aim to take your opponents by surprise! This shot is also incredibly powerful when aimed directly at your opponent.

Return Serve with Backspin

A well-executed version of this shot is highly effective and downright amusing.

Watch for a semi-high serve to come your way to execute this shot. Slice straight downward with your paddle when it appears soft and easy. The ball will rise softly into the air yet fall with a significant amount of sidespin. The ball should bounce directly to the side, making it difficult for your opponent to return it. The shot should fall on either side of the kitchen and bounce a foot off the ground and to the side if done correctly.

Evidently, this shot is notably risky. It might easily go out, into the net, or just be a typical return serve that accomplished nothing but raise your risk. The spin will be considerably more intense if you use a paddle with a fiberglass face.

Around-The-Post Shot

This is a very unusual, yet lethal shot. Given its rarity and grandeur, it's one of the most eye-catching shots. This shot is only possible if your opponent hits a hard crosscourt shot or dink that bounces far away from your side of the court. The trick here is to run with the ball in order to keep up with the tempo. You can strike the ball softly around the post as long as it has rebounded far enough out of the sideline. You may bask in the cheers that will erupt all around you.

Remember, if it hits the side post, it's a fault, even if it landed on the opposing team's courtside!

Spin Backhand Dink

If you're already familiar with a dinking stroke, you might consider upgrading to something more unique. This shot only works if you're making a crosscourt dink shot with your backhand. Right-handed players will be on the left side of the court, while left-handed players will be on the right.

If you're confident enough, this is a great shot to employ. To get some backspin on the ball, cut below it. Your opponent will most likely see the shot in motion and be prepared for it, but it doesn't mean mistakes won't occur.

This shot is deceiving since the dink is generally gentle, but the backspin changes everything. A typical error with this shot is hitting it too high. You might want to stick with a standard cross-court dink if you're up against big players with long wingspans.

Stacking

Stacking is a Pickleball doubles technique meant to shift players (partners) out of their "conventional" starting court positions and into a re-arranged position on the court, in order to acquire an advantage or desired result during the rally.

Stacking on the Serve

When stacking on the serve, both serving partners are normally positioned side-by-side (as if stacked) on the even or odd side to start the rally. Once the serve is delivered, the server (the one closest to the centerline) will slide across to the other side of the court.

Return-of-Serve Stacking

Both team players will begin the rally on the same courtside when stacking on the return-of-serve (odd side or even side). A player who returns the serve will be at or slightly behind the baseline. The partner of the return-of-server will be placed beyond the sideline (out-of-bounds) but near the NVZ line. The returner will move over to the other side after returning the serve, while the partner near the NVZ line will simply slip into the volley position on the close court.

TIPs:

- Because the return-of-server must return the serve and then cover the other side of the court, the return should be shot deep and high enough to allow them to cover the open court.
- When a team is stacking, it is usually easy to lose track of who should be serving and/or returning serve, and from where on the court the serve or return should be accomplished.
- To avoid any confusion, it's crucial to (1) keep track of the current score, and (2) remember which person on the stacking

team started the game as the first server. When the score is even, the first server should serve from the even side of the court; when their score is odd, the first server should serve from the odd side of the court.

- When the stacking team returns serve, the player who began the game serving (the first server) will return the serve from the even side when their score is even, and from the odd side when their score is odd.

The stacking player arrangement approach is mostly employed in tournaments. Except when players are training for tournaments, it is rarely used in social play. For all rallies, the stacking player arrangement method retains the same player (player A) on the ad court and the same player (player B) on the deuce court.

When and How to Employ the Stacking Method

While a left-handed player is playing alongside a right-handed player, both forehands should be in the center at all times, both when serving and receiving. In the stacking configuration, the left-handed player will be allocated to the deuce (even) court, while the right-handed player will be assigned to the ad (odd) court. Many rallies come to an end when the ball becomes too high. This configuration assures that if a ball in the center of the court rises too high, a forehand will smash it.

When a player with limited mobility is paired with a partner with excellent mobility, assign the player with limited mobility to the deuce court and the player with excellent mobility to the ad court. This assumes that the athlete with outstanding mobility is right-handed. Why? A right-handed player with high mobility can move and field a shot going diagonally right considerably more easily than a right-handed player with good mobility can move and field a shot going diagonally left.

Conclusion

Pickleball improvement requires time and effort, but you'll get off to a good start by adopting the strong Pickleball strategies from this book.

There are so many different ways to strike that it might be difficult for a beginner. Nevertheless, even the most experienced players will admit that understanding the foundations of the game is a vital first step in achieving Pickleball success, as well as finding the appropriate shots to fight back in a tight Pickleball location.

Competing in tournaments or leagues is a terrific method to go from the best player to outstanding. If you want to become a great player, you need to play against and compete against the best. Starting to compete is perhaps the most important choice you'll ever make. You may see where you stand and how far you've progressed by taking part in a competition.

Practicing against superior opponents will help you improve as a player. Both what to do and not do may be gleaned from their experiences. With practice, you'll be able to put the approaches in this book into action.

Thank You

Thank you for buying my book and I hope you enjoyed it. If you found any value in this book I would really appreciate it if you'd take a minute to post a review about this book. I check all my reviews and love to get feedback.

This is the real reward for me knowing that I'm helping others. If you know anyone who may enjoy this book, please share the message and gift it to them.

Other Books By Author

CLICK HERE TO SEE OTHER AUTHORS' BOOKS ON AMAZON!

About Author

I'm Dennis Hall, and I'm a PPR-certified pickleball coach. I've started playing and coaching pickleball for many years. My Queens, NY meeting club specializes in offering workshops for newbies and intermediate. My previous experiences involve coaching junior tennis at the school level, competing in Many Senior Pickleball League and earning a gold medal in doubles matches.

I've coached hundreds of students how to play pickleball from the ground up and led students through the difficulties of progressing from beginner to intermediate. PICKLEBALL BOOK FOR BEGINNERS was written because I understand how difficult it is for individuals to begin in the game. This book is chock-full of tips, instructions, and resources. It is, in my opinion, a must-read for anybody interested in learning how to play pickleball.

Made in the USA
Coppell, TX
21 October 2023